That's the Swedish way!

Model nation, world conscience, the country that protects its citizens from the cradle to the grave…

…yes, Sweden carries a variety of international labels. Most of them allude to our proficiency, organizational skills, neatness and slightly naive, officious nature. The international cliché of Sweden portrays us as nation of capable, well-groomed but also mildly phlegmatic and boring souls, who not only obsessively clean and polish our own idyllic little Nordic nest, but are also presumptuous enough to have opinions about how other, bigger, more important nations should run their affairs.

This image certainly contains a grain of truth. Sweden is a small Nordic nation that, in the space of a century, has transformed itself from a poor, underdeveloped agrarian country into one of the world's most modern and sophisticated welfare states and industrialized nations: truly a feat worthy of taking pride in. Indeed, we are proficient, hard working, conscientious and well-groomed – well, perhaps a little boring and officious too, for that matter. To an outsider, the Swedes at first glance may also appear to be a somewhat shy, withdrawn, anonymous people. But don't let yourself be fooled by this surface. Beneath it lurks madness, sensuality, sentimentality and – not least – a well-disguised national pride and self-confidence.

Then, of course, we have all those S words - sex, sin, suicide, socialism… but more on that elsewhere in "Sweden & Swedes"…

Claes Britton

Culture:
From folklore to hiphop

International observers who encounter Sweden and Swedish culture for the first time are often amazed at the richness of our cultural heritage, regardless of whether their interests are painting, architecture, opera, poetry or contemporary design, fashion, music or gastronomy. How could so few people, so far away from major cultural centers, have managed to accomplish so much? they often wonder.

We Swedes have always been remarkably quick and diligent at snapping up impressions from outside sources. Our national creative culture can be described as based on a skillful reshaping of impulses borrowed from other, larger cultures. But deep down is our very own soul: simplicity, ingenuity, melancholy and an eternal longing to return to our modest, innocent, rural origins.

Literature:
In childhood's light and Strindberg's shadow

It is customary to say that Sweden's modern literary history began in the 18th century with the mystic philosopher Emanuel Swedenborg. During the late 18th century our national poet, Carl Michael Bellman, composed his peerless life-affirming drinking songs and idyllic pastorales. Late in the 19th century, a number of important Swedish authors emerged, but by now they have almost all faded into the shadow of the demonic, ever-controversial, multi-talented August Strindberg, whose international reputation rests mainly on his role as one of the most influential dramatists in literary history.

During the first half of the 20th century, a strong current emerged that came to distinguish our Swedish literary heritage: proletarian prose. This school includes a number of authors – including a few women – with similar backgrounds and literary motifs: poor, self-taught farm children and workers, who used poetic realism to portray their own difficult upbringing and, in the process, left behind a record of Sweden's transformation from a timeless agrarian country to a modern industrialized society, often against a backdrop of nature lyricism.

Eyvind Johnson and Harry Martinson (who shared the 1974 Nobel Prize in Literature), Ivar Lo-Johansson and Vilhelm Moberg are only a few of the biggest names from this generation of writers.

After a long period of writing for a more or less isolated and national literary market, today more and more Swedish writers are seeing their works translated into a growing number of foreign languages. Works by many of the contemporary Swedish writers who have reaped international success can be classified as popular literature. They include detective and adventure book authors Henning Mankell, Jan Guillou, Håkan Nesser and Liza Marklund. In more strictly literary genres, too, Swedish authors have made breakthroughs in recent years. Two of the foremost names are prosaist Per Olov Enquist and poet Tomas Tranströmer, both of them recipients of numerous international awards.

Another defining Swedish literary tradition is the children's book. The great name in this field is of course Astrid Lindgren (1907–2002). Her classics about Pippi Longstocking, Emil, Mardie, Karlson on the Roof, Ronia the Robber's Daughter, the Brothers Lionheart and many more have been translated to almost a hundred languages and sold by the millions worldwide. In Sweden, her six-decade-long writing career gave her the status of national treasure. Her books have influenced – and

Two Swedish literary icons: August Strindberg and Astrid Lindgren's Pippi Longstocking; bestselling author Henning Mankell.

Women on the silver screen: Harriet Andersson in *Summer With Monika* and Oksana Akinshina in *Lilya 4-ever*; classic nymph from Dalarna by Anders Zorn.

continue to influence – generations of Swedes, not only in childhood but throughout their lives.

Film & stage:
Is there life after Bergman?

There is no doubt that Swedish cinema of the 1950s and 1960s was the main "villain" behind the still-thriving myth of Sweden as a country populated by exquisitely beautiful, vigorously healthy, sexually liberated blondes who nude-bathe in the white summer night. To say that the films of Ingmar Bergman, Vilgot Sjöman (*I Am Curious Yellow*) and Arne Mattsson (*One Summer of Happiness*) from this period, with their episodes of nudity, triggered an international sensation hardly suffices as a description.

The importance of Ingmar Bergman in Swedish and world cinematic history is of course impossible to overstate. During his 60-year career as a film and theater director, Bergman has not only dominated Swedish stage and screen, but also perhaps more than any other individual he has influenced the international image of Sweden and Swedishness, both visually and culturally.

Like many other branches of Swedish culture, over the past decade Swedish film has become increasingly international in its expression, and its practitioners have also begun to achieve considerable success abroad. The best-known name internationally among today's Swedish film directors is Lasse Hallström, who relocated many years ago to Hollywood, where he is pursuing a career along with such Swedish actors as his wife Lena Olin as well as Stellan Skarsgård and Peter Stormare – the latter being internationally the best known name. In a younger generation, Lukas Moodysson has attracted international attention with his films *Show Me Love*, *Together* and *Lilya 4-ever*. A new element of Swedish filmmaking is a number of gifted young directors with immigrant backgrounds, making films about what is usually called "the new Sweden." The pioneer in this genre is Josef Fares, several of whose comedies have been both artistically and commercially successful. Another niche where Sweden has made its mark internationally in recent years is commercials and music videos.

On the live stage – theater, musicals, dance and other shows – Sweden also has plenty to offer. The capital, Stockholm, prides itself of being the world's most "theater-packed" city. The Royal Dramatic Theater and the Royal Opera, two national stages of the highest international caliber,

frequently have spectacular premieres and guest appearances on their repertoire. In recent years the world-famous Cullberg Ballet, with contemporary dance on its repertoire, has faced competition from a number of dance ensembles and from such choreographers as Kenneth Kvarnström, Virpi Pahkinen and Cristina Caprioli.

Art:
From naked nymphs to female video artists

The history of Swedish art, like Swedish culture in general, is comparatively young and modest compared to the great European civilizations to our south. Such historical epochs as classic antiquity and the Renaissance are simply not represented at our northerly latitudes.

The history of Swedish art can be said to begin, at least in an international perspective, late in the 18th century with portrait painter Alexander Roslin and sculptor Tobias Sergel. But actually it was not until the late 19th century, during the National Romantic epoch, that Swedish painting took off in earnest. Just as in literature and architecture, a love of – not to say a worship of – nature is one of the sustaining motifs in Swedish art from this period. The great national painters of the era around the turn of the 20th century – Anders Zorn, Bruno Liljefors, Carl Larsson and many more – portray an eternal Nordic longing for nature and for a pure, simple life.

During the 1960s and early 1970s, Sweden and especially its capital of Stockholm put themselves on the world map of modern art when Moderna museet opened under the leadership of the legendary Pontus Hultén (later director of the Centre Pompidou in Paris and other major international museums). For some 15 years, Stockholm was one of the most important meeting places of the international art world. Today Moderna museet is recognized as having been one of the main trend-setters among modern art museums of that era. One heritage from that period is the museum's permanent collection of international 20th century art, especially pop art, which is counted among the most outstanding in the world. There are great hopes that Moderna museet will begin a new era of greatness under its director Lars Nittve, who was recruited back to Stockholm after spearheading the launch of the Tate Modern in London.

The late 20th and early 21st century has also witnessed an encouraging breakthrough for Swedish artists in the interna-

Contemporary Swedish sounds: Howlin' Pelle of The Hives and The Knife.

tional arena – a trend that parallels the one we have seen in music, design, cinema and literature. A striking number of these artists are women, many active in photography and video art. Among many names worth remembering are Annika von Hausswolff, Annika Eriksson Rixon, Ann-Sofie Sidén and Maria Misenberger.

Music:
A musical miracle in minor key

It is widely reported that little Sweden is the world's third largest music-exporting nation, "beaten" only by the two musical superpowers, the United States and Great Britain.

It is difficult to verify the truth of such a comparison. What is clear is that Sweden's success in the international music market, especially in the past decade, has been astonishing. Our country is sometimes described as a music factory, ceaselessly churning out new "product" in every genre from sing-along pop to death metal. Especially striking is Swedish achievements in the most commercial types of pop music, where not only Swedish performers but perhaps above all Swedish songwriters and producers have won world-wide repu-

tations. The Swedish commercial sound has become a global recipe for success. Surprisingly often, lurking behind the biggest international superstars are Swedish creative teams.

As in many other cultural fields, in today's globalized world it is difficult to articulate exactly what is typically Swedish about this sound. Instead it is more a matter of Swedish music creators who are unusually quick and adept at snapping up international influences and then, with great pizzazz, reformulating them into their own, highly "contagious" music. Some people say that Swedish performers and songwriters have a special feeling for strong melodies, which in turn may be based on our tradition of melancholy folk ballads in a minor key. Another explanation is our municipal music schools, which from the 1960s onward have made it possible for children from all social classes to begin making music at an early age. There may be something to both of these theories.

One thing that is certain is that the pop music group ABBA, with their unique string of hits during the 1970s and early 1980s, played a role equivalent to that of tennis star Björn Borg in Swedish sports. ABBA opened international doors to the Swedish music industry and other Swedish performers.

Equally apparent is that in Sweden, music has deep popular roots. This

"Self Portrait 1999" by Annika von Hausswolff.

Light colors, simplicity and low-key, sophisticated elegance are distinguishing qualities of contemporary Swedish design.

applies not only to pop music but also to the entire musical spectrum from folk to jazz to opera. For example, Sweden is said to have by far the largest per capita number of amateur choirs in the world.

Fashion & design:
Minimalistic extravagance

The past decade has witnessed a creative rebirth and an international breakthrough for Swedish culture in various fields. However, Sweden's success in contemporary design has attracted the greatest attention. The impression is that Sweden came out of nowhere to a role today as the world's third-ranking major power in international product and interior design – after Italy and Great Britain.

This is an impression that ignores history. Sweden has a long and proud history in art handicrafts and its modern incarnation, industrial design. Since the late 1920s, when the expression "Swedish Grace" was coined, and until the mid-1960s, Sweden was a world leader in both design and architecture.

In our modern history, the 20-year period of decline between 1965 and 1985 is, instead, the exception. In the late 1980s, such designers as Thomas Sandell,

Pia Wallén, Mats Theselius and Jonas Bohlin, together with a number of small, progressive producers, introduced themselves to an international audience and soon engineered a breakthrough in international design and lifestyle media. This new generation of design bore the same features that had distinguished what was known worldwide in the first half of the 20th century as "Swedish Grace" and "Swedish Modern": simplicity, practicality, a light palette of colors, respect for natural materials and a characteristic low-keyed elegance spiced with humor and ingenuity.

In recent years the Swedish capital of Stockholm in particular has become an important meeting place for international design, in some respects fully comparable with such design metropolises as London and Milan. The traditional Swedish furniture and art handicrafts industry centered in Småland province, southern Sweden, has also latched onto this new current and has begun to show its mettle internationally as a creator of contemporary design. The biggest and strongest of these Småland-based companies, in a superdivision all its own, is of course IKEA, but that is another story, worth telling in its own right…

Traditional folk art is back in style, also as a source of inspiration for today's Swedish designers.

Since the late 1980s, Swedish restaurant culture and gastronomy have soared in both quality and international acclaim.

In fashion and textiles, Sweden also has a proud tradition to live up to. A growing number of gifted young fashion designers have established their own brands in the market. So far, however, these designers have found it much more difficult to achieve commercial success than their colleagues in furniture and industrial products. Sweden, a small market for artistic fashion, is instead dominated by successful low- and medium-price chains, of which H&M is naturally by far the most prominent market player.

Folk art:
Tradition is trend

Traditional Swedish handicrafts bear clear witness of our simple, rustic Nordic origins in their expressions, colors, shapes and choices of material. They meanwhile exhibit the same traits that have made Swedish design a global brand: simplicity, clean lines, forcefulness, harmony and homage to nature.

Physically, Sweden is a large and far-flung country. The variations in handicraft expressions are sizeable as we move from the fells of Lapland with their traditional Sami crafts and southward all the way to the fertile plains of Skåne province, especially well known for their bold, colorful traditional textiles. Different regions specialize in different types of handicrafts – wood and birch crafts, wrought iron, woven baskets, ceramics, leather goods and textiles. Especially rich and lively is the history of traditional handicrafts in Dalarna region, with their characteristic and original *kurbits* style of floral paintings. This north central province is also the birthplace of Sweden's best known national symbol, the *kurbits*-painted wooden Dala horse.

In recent years, traditional art handicrafts have experienced something of a renaissance in the younger generations as well. A number of contemporary fashion and interior designers have contributed to this revived interest by drawing inspiration from traditional Swedish folk art in their design work.

Gastronomy:
Don't laugh at the Swedish chef!

In recent decades, Swedish gastronomy and restaurant culture have undergone a metamorphosis. As late as the mid-1980s, our Swedish cuisine was still provincial and was more or less uninteresting from an international perspective – based on our domestic home cooking tradition, with its weighty heritage of peasant food like meatballs, stuffed cabbage rolls, potato dumplings and pickled herring.

Since then, we have been in the midst of a lengthy restaurant and food boom, which still shows no signs at all of weakening. On the contrary, our Swedish culinary tradition has opened up wide to impressions from throughout the world. Young Swedish chefs have taken their gastronomic inventiveness to ever-greater heights, transcending culinary borders without forgetting our own rural origins. Among creative young Swedes, the profession of chef de cuisine has earned star status. In the increasingly popular international gastronomic contests that are the world championships and the Olympics of culinary culture, Swedes have celebrated major triumphs both in team and individual competitions.

Stockholm's wide array of restaurants has recently become one of the city's most important international attractions.

This highly publicized restaurant boom is not restricted to the capital, however. Virtually everywhere in the country, the gastronomically inclined can now find restaurants and country inns that are well worth a detour.

Nature:
Small nation, great country

With only nine million people, Sweden is a small nation in terms of population – smaller than Belgium and only half as big as the Netherlands. Perhaps this is why foreigners are often surprised when they realize the geographic size of our country. Physically, Sweden is one of the largest countries in Western Europe – nearly the same size as Spain or France and larger than California.

Because of its large area and limited number of inhabitants, Sweden is one of Europe's most sparsely populated countries. Yet it is worth noting that nearly 90 percent of Sweden's population lives in the southern part of the country. In Norrland, which accounts for nearly 60 percent of Sweden's area, fewer than a million people live. From the vast open spaces of Norrland – sometimes referred to as the last wildness in Western Europe – come most of the enormous natural resources of forests, ores and hydroelectric power on which the country based its industrialization. About one sixth of Sweden's area lies north of the Arctic Circle, in the region known as Nordkalotten ("The Northern Skull-cap" of Europe), which also includes portions of Norway, Finland and Russia.

In all, more than half of Sweden's area consists of forests, mainly coniferous (evergreens). Some 16 percent of the country consists of mountains and fells. Nearly 10 percent is lakes, rivers and wetlands, while only 8 percent is cultivated land.

The warm Gulf Stream, which flows past the west coast of Norway, is what makes it possible for such a large proportion of Sweden and the rest of the Scandinavian peninsula to be inhabitable and cultivable at all. Areas at similar latitudes elsewhere in the world – for example in Canada, Alaska, Greenland and Siberia – consist largely of uninhabited tundra.

Scenery:
From barren fells to blazing meadows

Sweden is famous, especially among the Swedes themselves, for its natural beauty. We Swedes love our natural scenery with an almost religious intensity.

The country's great length from north to south – more than 1,600 kilometers, or 1,000 miles – makes the contrasts between its southern, central and northern parts dramatic. In the far north is the vast Lapland wilderness with its treeless fells, low wind-blown forests and inaccessible wetlands. The Scandinavian mountain chain runs roughly north and south along the western border of the country, like a backbone between Sweden and Norway. An overwhelming majority of the rest of northern and central Sweden is covered with deep coniferous forests, interspersed with blue lake systems and rushing rivers that run from the snow-clad peaks of the west down toward the Baltic Sea coast.

Along the eastern coast is a diversity of unique natural areas. They include the remarkable High Coast in the north – which is included on the UNESCO World Heritage List – and the unique Stockholm, St. Anne

Under the traditional "common right of access," everyone in Sweden enjoys unique freedom to move around and enjoy nature.

and Västervik archipelagoes with their tens of thousands of mainly uninhabited islands, isles and skerries. The west coast of Sweden runs northward to bare, pink-shaded islands that extend toward the Norwegian fjords. In the Baltic Sea off the east coast of Sweden are two major islands, Gotland and Öland, both unique in their natural scenery, with spiny limestone coasts and flowering beachside meadows, heaths and bare limestone plains, boasting a richness of species otherwise found in far more southerly climes.

Skåne extends across the southern end of the country. It is Sweden's richest and most fertile agricultural province, with rolling plains, gently rounded hills, murmuring deciduous forests and endless sandy beaches.

So large is our country, and so few are the Swedes, that wild natural scenery is within reach of everyone – a priceless luxury, but also a self-evident right that is free of charge.

Characteristic of our northerly natural scenery is the radical changes of season. The landscape really sheds its skin and changes its garb four times a year, with constant shifts in the strong nuances of color.

Environmental concerns:
All for the love of nature

Love and respect for Nordic nature is a key element of the Swedish soul and modern society. In Sweden there is an ancient and globally unique law known as the "common right of access," which gives everyone the right to move around freely (as well as to raise a tent, pick berries, mushrooms and flowers and so on) in nature – even on private property – as long as they are not within sight or hearing range of a residence. The basic principle of this right is "freedom under responsibility" – a self-evident obligation not to harm nature by leaving behind trash, breaking tree branches, being careless with fires and so on.

As a consequence of the Swedes' intimate relationship with nature, we realized at an early stage that natural resources are not infinite. Since the 1970s, Sweden has been among the leading countries both in protecting our own nature and working in the international arena to protect the global environment.

We can report with great pride that today Sweden has cleaner air, purer water and healthier forests than 20 years ago. Many once-endangered plant and animal species have been able to recover, thanks to active efforts from the authorities and from the public. One clearly visible proof of this positive trend is that the waters in the midst of the royal capital, Stockholm, are now healthy enough both to swim and fish in.

Internationally, Sweden has been active for decades in the global environmental efforts of the UN and other transnational organizations. Since Sweden's accession to the European Union in 1995, an important part of this international environmental work has occurred in the EU, where Sweden and its fellow Nordic member nations belong to the most progressive wing on environmental issues.

Midnight sun & northern light:
When the sun never sets

Sweden's northerly geographic location gives the country an extreme climate, nevertheless made gentler by the warm Gulf Stream that runs nearby in the North Atlantic Ocean. Foreign visitors often find the light conditions prevailing in our country even more extreme. In fact, the Nordic light has become one of Sweden's foremost international tourist attractions.

The midnight sun and the *aurora borealis* attract visitors to the far north.

During the spring, the days become longer and brighter, culminating in late June when the sun shines around the clock in the northern part of the country. Darkness sets in for only a few hours in the southern regions, and then it is more like a kind of mystical twilight. These bright nights occur throughout Sweden from late May into late July. In Lapland, the midnight sun is a phenomenon that attracts hordes of visitors from all over the globe every year.

In recent years, the opposite of summer's "white nights" – the compact Nordic winter darkness – has also become a tourist attraction in its own right, though on a more modest scale. Visitors from afar travel nowadays to Lapland to experience total winter darkness, massive silence and severe cold, with temperatures dropping to minus 30 degrees Celsius or lower. They can also enjoy the mighty colored-light symphony known as the *aurora borealis* (northern lights) playing across the Arctic winter sky. It is a visual phenomenon that occurs due to the earth's magnetism.

AVERAGE TEMPERATURES	IN JANUARY		IN JULY	
Malmö	– 0.2° C	(+31.6° F)	+16.8° C	(62.2° F)
Stockholm	– 2.8° C	(+27.0°F)	+17.2°C	(63.0°F)
Kiruna	–16.0°C	(+ 3.2° F)	+12.8°C	(55.0°F)
DAYLIGHT (APPROX. VALUES)	JANUARY 1		JULY 1	
Malmö	7 hours		17 hours	
Stockholm	6 hours		18 hours	
Kiruna	0 hours		24 hours	

Brown bears and lynx are two of the many wild species in Sweden's forests.

Wild animals:
In company of moose, bears, wolves & lynx

In the forests and wildernesses that cover two thirds of Sweden live a large number of wild animal species. Many of these, which were previously rare or actually endangered, have fortunately rocovered in recent years, usually as a result of long-term efforts to protect them and improve their environment and living conditions.

Sweden is best known for the moose (or elk), our unofficial national animal and popular motif on all imaginable tourist souvenirs. The moose is one of what could be called the Swedish answer to Africa's Big Five. The other four "members" of this quintet are all predatory animals: the wolverine, which lives mainly in Lapland and hunts reindeer, among others; the wolf, a previously endangered species that has re-covered and now shows up even in south-ern Sweden; the brown bear, found mostly in the northwestern forests and fells; and the lynx, the Nordic region's own big cat – a species that is now thriving in large forested areas throughout the country.

Linnaeus:
He broke the code of nature

Carl von Linné (1707–78), born Linnaeus – the name by which he is still known in English-speaking countries – was a great Swedish physician and botanist. In those days, botany was part of medicine. He is primarily famous for his *Systema naturae*, a classification system for plants, animals and minerals. Linné carried out several well known journeys in Sweden, among others to the provinces of Lapland,

Carl von Linné: Botanist as revolutionary

Dalarna and Skåne, publishing detailed reports on the structure of their natural systems. His students, sometimes called his "disciples," also traveled around the world on similar journeys of discovery – to Japan, China, the Americas, Australia, Arabia and the Arctic Ocean. Only in recent years have scientists been able to fully appreciate the breadth of Linné's brilliant research career. For example, he is considered perhaps the most important forerunner of Darwin. His stringent stan-dards of empirical evidence for all conclu-sions were also important in the general development of natural science research methods.

Society:
In the choice between two roads, we traveled the third...

The "Golden Middle Way" – this Swedish phrase says something about a nation that has always honored compromise, understanding, concord and the less bad of two imperfect alternatives. It was perhaps no coincidence that Sweden managed to remain in the middle when 20th century Europe split itself into capitalist and communist blocs.

Especially in American propaganda, Sweden in the 1950s, 60s and 70s was often portrayed as a half-communist nation where the freedom of the citizenry was tightly restricted. This is a false mythological image. Sweden is a thoroughly democratized nation and a solid market economy.

However, it is true that Sweden – perhaps to a greater extent than any other Western country – has applied socialist elements in its redistribution policy, led by a Social Democratic Party that ruled the country from the 1930s until 2006 with only a few interruptions. The prosperity that Sweden built up during the 20th century was distributed among the population in the form of large tax-financed systems of education, health care, child and elder care, parental insurance, pensions and various general allowances. The consequence has been a society with narrower economic gaps between the social classes than in comparable countries.

This classic welfare state has been referred to internationally as the "middle way," the "third way" or the "Swedish model" – the latter expression originally describing the centralized negotiations between Swedish employers and the country's strong unions, which secured crucial stability in the labor market for several decades as the welfare state expanded.

Care & welfare:
From the cradle to the grave

The labor movement and other "popular movements" (temperance, women's rights etc.) gained major influence at an early stage. In the 1920s, the Social Democrats came to power for the first time. During the 1930s, Sweden began to build up what then-Prime Minister Per Albin Hansson called "the home of the people" (*folkhem*). Its vision was to lift Sweden out of poverty once and for all, and to build a society where all citizens, regardless of gender, class, social origins and other circumstances, would be guaranteed basic economic security by the public sector. This Swedish "home of the people" would not be dependent on charity, but instead would be financed by a tax system in which the well-to-do would bear the main economic burden. The principle was "from each according to ability, to each according to needs." One of several labels for this social welfare structure was the "third way" – a narrow, previously untrodden path between capitalism and socialism.

It was mainly during the 1950s and 1960s, a period of unparalleled economic growth in Sweden, that the world's most generous tax-financed social welfare system was built up. This included a long series of reforms, many of them later emulated elsewhere in the world.

"The country that protects its citizens from the cradle to the grave" – this is yet another of the expressions by which Sweden is sometimes described internationally, often with a slightly sarcastic undertone. There is a lot of truth to this image. What characterizes the Swedish system is that the public sector has taken over large portions of the responsibility for its citizens' economic security that have otherwise traditionally rested with the family.

It all begins right from infancy, with public maternity care centers, and then continues with day care centers and preschools. In recent years, private and family-cooperative day care centers have been allowed into the market, but financing is still largely provided by the public sector, with day care fees on a sliding scale adjusted to the parents' income, up to a certain maximum. Schooling is free, in other words tax-financed – not only in the nine-year compulsory school and the three-year upper secondary school, but also at university and college level, where the government offers study loans so that young people from all social classes can afford to study.

The health insurance system guarantees all inhabitants virtually free health care and subsidized medicines and dental care. Sickness benefits – and parental insurance benefits – offset lost income (up to a certain ceiling) when a person is absent from work due to illness or parenthood. Elder care, too, is almost entirely financed by the public sector. For the elderly there is also a public basic pension as well as an income-based supplementary pension. Sweden also has publicly financed systems of housing allowances, unemployment benefits and social assistance, among others. The noble ambition of this social welfare safety net is that every Swede, regardless of ability or circumstances, should always be able to rely on the public sector to provide at least the most basic needs.

In recent years, Sweden's massive security systems have often been under heavy eco-

The Swedish Parliament Building in Stockholm.

nomic pressures, especially during slowdowns, with such problems as waiting lists for elective health care, shortages of personnel, deficits in pension systems etc. With an aging population – due to ever longer life expectancy – and large generations retiring in the years ahead, one major political and economic challenge will be to develop systems that can continue to guarantee economic security and well-being to everyone.

HEAD OF STATE: Since 1973 King Carl XVI Gustaf, married since 1976 to Queen Silvia; three children, of whom the oldest, Victoria, is Crown Princess.

HEAD OF GOVERNMENT: Fredrik Reinfeldt, prime minister in a non-socialist majority government.

Democracy today:
Can we make a difference?

Sweden is a representative democracy, whose legislature is the Swedish Parliament (Riksdag), with 349 members in one chamber. Parliamentary elections are held every four years. After the 2006 election, twelve years of Social Democratic government ended when the four Alliance parties – the Moderates (formerly Conservatives), Liberals, Center (formerly Agrarians) and Christian Democrats – formed a government. The prime minister is the 41-year chairman of the Moderates. The Social

Parliamentary election, September 2006: percentage of votes and number of seats by party (the threshold for entering Parliament is 4.0 percent)

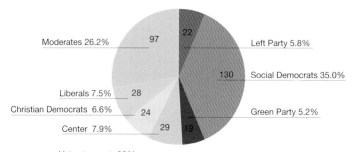

Moderates 26.2% — 97
Left Party 5.8% — 22
Social Democrats 35.0% — 130
Green Party 5.2% — 19
Center 7.9% — 29
Christian Democrats 6.6% — 24
Liberals 7.5% — 28

Voter turnout: 82%.
Women Members of Parliament: 47%

Swedish citizens 18 and over are entitled to vote in parliamentary and local elections. Foreign citizens who have been registered as Swedish residents for at least three years may vote in municipal and county council elections.

Equal rights and shared responsibility for men and women in child-rearing are major goals of Swedish family policy.

Democrats, who ruled Sweden for most of the 20th century and enjoyed a uniquely dominant position of power over national policy compared to other Western European countries, turned in one of their worst election performances ever. In the new Parliament they are in opposition along with the Left Party (ex-communists) and the Green Party.

In recent decades, Swedish democracy has struggled with a problem that is common in the Western world: declining political involvement among the population. Political parties have found it increasingly difficult to recruit members, especially in younger age categories. Voter turnout, which was previously at an exceptionally high level in international terms, has been falling for some time. In the 2006 parliamentary election, however, turnout rose somewhat to a bit above 80 percent. The turnout in elections to the European Parliament is, however, far lower than this, around 50 percent.

Despite these figures, the Swedish democratic tradition must be regarded as very strong. Our society can be described as thoroughly democratized, with strong democratic elements not only in national, regional and local politics, but also at schools, workplaces, in various interest organizations and in other segments of society.

Equal rights:
Not only all men should be equal...

Sweden was not among the pioneering countries in introducing women's suffrage. However, since women gained the right to vote in 1921, efforts to achieve gender equality have progressed further in many sectors of Swedish society than in perhaps any other country.

The main principle of Swedish gender equality efforts is that all people, both men and women, should be economically independent of any other person for their living. Another important ambition is that men and women, as far as possible, should share equal responsibility for family economic support and child-rearing. Sweden has the world's most generous parental insurance system, which enables parents to be at home with their children for 16 months of paid leave. Sweden was also the first country in the world to turn one (now expanded to two) of these months of paid leave into mandatory "daddy months."

Generally speaking, the ambition to improve the position of women in society has been an important driving force in the expansion of the Swedish welfare state. Thus the public sector has taken over a large proportion of responsibilities that once traditionally rested with women, mainly child and elder care. As a consequence of this policy Sweden today has a very high percentage of women in the labor market – 76 percent as compared to 80 percent of men. In the upper reaches of the national establishment, gender equality efforts have made major progress in politics and public administration. In private business, the trend toward greater gender equality has also shifted into higher gear in recent years, among other things due to tough demands for a substantially larger share of women on corporate boards of directors.

Today there is a whole set of laws and ordinances aimed at guaranteeing equal rights, equal pay for the same work and prohibitions on discrimination and sexual harassment etc. Many of these laws apply to the conditions in the labor market, with compliance being monitored by the Equal Opportunities Ombudsman.

Sweden also has very far-reaching legislation and practices aimed at banning discrimination and unfavorable special treatment of people due to their ethnic background, physical or mental disabilities or sexual orientation. We also have far-reaching laws aimed at ensuring the rights of children not only in society, but also in the family. For example, Sweden triggered international controversy in the 1970s when it became the first country in the world to forbid parents from spanking their children.

The JAS 39 Gripen combat aircraft: Made in Sweden.

Transparency & influence:
The see-through society

Openness is yet another of the fundamental principles of Sweden's public sector. The opportunity to examine how our politicians and public agencies exercise their power is a self-evident civil right in Sweden. The "principle of publicity," which goes further in Sweden than in most countries, not only makes all written business and all correspondence (even e-mails) to and from our government ministries, municipalities and public agencies available to the press and the general public, but legislation also requires public agencies to provide this information in easily usable form and free of charge.

Internationally, the Swedish principle of publicity is considered so radical that it has been among the constant sources of friction in the EU, where Swedish representatives have often encountered resistance and lack of understanding when they have advocated greater openness and "transparency."

Another important guarantee of openness in the Swedish public sector is the well-known ombudsman system, which has actually been adopted in a number of other countries. The offices of the various ombudsmen are publicly financed agencies, entrusted with safeguarding the interests of individual citizens and population groups as well as overseeing how other public agencies exercise their power.

In the Swedish private business sector, too, compared with many other countries, there is a strong tradition of openness, information and employee co-determination. For example, legislation entitles the trade unions to representation on the boards of directors of all stock exchange-listed companies.

Peace & neutrality:
In defense of peace

Non-alignment in peacetime, neutrality in wartime – this is the security doctrine on which Swedish foreign and defense policy has been based in modern times. Without doubt, this doctrine has been successful in its main purpose, since it was one of the most important reasons why Sweden managed to stay outside both world wars during the 20th century. Meanwhile Sweden has been active in world political efforts to keep the peace, especially in the United Nations. Sweden and

Once homogeneously Lutheran, Sweden has rapidly become a country of many religious cultures.

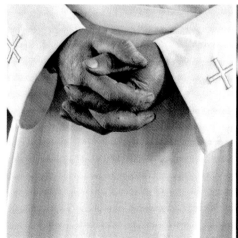

Swedish diplomats have also frequently acted as mediators in various conflicts. Well-known Swedish names in international peace efforts have included Dag Hammarskjöld (Secretary-General of the UN from 1953 to 1961), Raoul Wallenberg, Folke Bernadotte, Olof Palme and Hans Blix.

In recent years, since the collapse of the communist bloc, Swedish neutrality policy has been subjected to serious debate for the first time. Today Sweden is a long-time member of the EU, which was previously considered incompatible with neutrality. Some people also believe that Sweden should join the North Atlantic Treaty Organization (NATO), while others argue firmly that even in a new world security situation, non-participation in military alliances must remain a basic feature of Swedish foreign policy.

Swedish security policy is based on a strong defense system, according to the principle that Sweden must be strong enough to defend itself without relying on others. Sweden has a mainly conscript army, which has been cut back substantially in recent years, due to both the new world political situation and the general need to save money. Swedish defense policy is also based on a domestic arms industry that is dependent on exports for its survival. These arms exports are a continuous topic of emotional debate. The Swedish arms industry is prohibited from exporting to countries at war. Peace activists and other critics perceive this as hypocritical – after all, arms are made for fighting wars, they argue.

Religion:
What religion?

Sweden today would undoubtedly qualify as one of the world's least religious, most secularized countries. Like so much else in our country, this is a process that has occurred at a rapid pace, in less than a century. Until the late 19th century, the Swedes were a highly God-fearing, homogeneous Lutheran people. To say that the Church of Sweden – in our modern society – has lost its religious significance for most people and, like the monarchy, been

The new Swedes: Waves of immigration in recent decades have transformed Sweden into a multicultural society.

transformed into a purely ceremonial cultural heritage is perhaps an exaggeration, but not an especially big one.

Sweden broke with the Roman Catholic Church in the 16th century and has since been a highly Protestant country. For more than four centuries, the evangelical Lutheran Church, or Church of Sweden, was the official state church. This was true until the year 2000, when church and state separated after decades of debate.

Almost 80 percent of the Swedes still belong to the Church of Sweden. Nevertheless, for most Swedes the Church is an institution that they come into contact with mainly on ceremonial occasions such as christenings, confirmations (still fairly common), weddings and funerals.

Immigrants account for the biggest genuine religious reawakening in this country. With hundreds of thousands of "new Swedes" from different religions and cultures, Sweden today is far from homogeneously Lutheran, but is instead a multicultural nation in religious respects as well.

Immigration:
The new Swedes

The transformation of Swedish society during the past century has been dramatic in many ways. However, the question is

whether any other single phenomenon has triggered such a radical change as postwar immigration to Sweden.

Until World War II, immigration to Sweden was marginal. During the 19th century, Sweden was instead a country of emigration. No fewer than one fifth of the population emigrated between around 1850 and 1930, mainly to North America.

During the postwar period, large streams of immigrants arrived in Sweden in search of work and a livelihood – mainly from neighboring Nordic countries but also from southern Europe. In the 1980s, labor immigration faded as regulations tightened and was replaced by waves of refugees from countries outside the EU, and since then such immigration has remained at a very high international level in relation to the country's population. Today nearly 1.5 million people living in Sweden (16 percent) have immigrant backgrounds, meaning that they themselves were born abroad or they have two foreign-born parents.

In a very short time, this immigration has made Sweden a more international, open and multicultural country. Such a radical change has of course also created various difficulties, such as housing and cultural segregation, unemployment among certain immigrant groups and cultural frictions as well. But in an international comparison we have been relatively free of such malignant expressions as ethnic violence and populist xenophobic political parties at the national level.

Economy:
A call for innovation

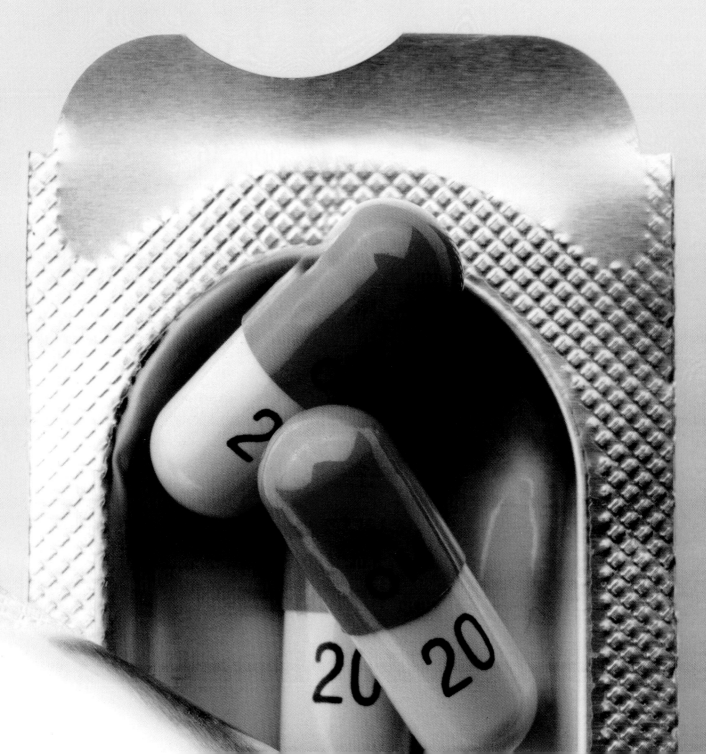

Sweden's evolution from a poor, backward agrarian country to a modern industrialized nation in the space of only half a century is internationally classified as an economic miracle, in many respects comparable with that of Japan. The outstanding export success of Swedish industry during the 20th century made possible the creation of the famous Swedish welfare state.

The prerequisites for this industrial revolution can be found in northern Sweden's enormous natural resources: forests, ore and hydroelectric power. But in Sweden there is also a proud tradition of inventiveness and entrepreneurship. Swedish industrialists did not content themselves with exploiting raw materials, but found innovative new ways of enhancing the value of these natural resources. A long series of ingenious Swedish inventions and innovations laid the foundation for Sweden's engineering, chemical/pharmaceutical and electrical industries, among others.

Today this heritage continues in such high-tech, research-intensive sectors as information technology (IT) and biomedicine – fields in which Sweden has long been among the world leaders. Over the decades, the Swedish business sector has undergone a process of frequently painful transformations. Manufacturing jobs have vanished abroad as companies have moved portions of their production to low-wage countries. Many of the largest Swedish corporations have also been sold or merged with multinational groups. Today, as one century ago, the future hope of Swedish industry rests with inventiveness, fresh thinking and entrepreneurship – the ability to find new solutions in response to a new reality.

Traditional industry:
Prosperity started in the frozen forest

In the late 19th century, railroads and electricity made northern Sweden's enormous natural resources of forests, ore and hydroelectric power accessible as the Swedish industrial revolution took off in earnest. On the European Continent, industrialization had begun earlier, and there was insatiable demand for iron ore, timber and paper. At this time, Norrland (the northern three-fifths of Sweden) was a land of pioneers, where industrialists were making money hand over fist. Money earned by the "forest barons" of Norrland directly or indirectly built a large proportion of the sumptuous, turn-of-the-century stone façade buildings that dominate central Stockholm even today. During and after both of the world wars, Sweden's industry rose to new heights as belligerent nations shouted for more Swedish raw materials and products.

The period around the turn of the 20th century also witnessed the establishment of numerous Swedish industrial companies that, even today, remain at the core of the Swedish business sector. Most of these

The Volvo YCC, with many innovation solutions, designed by women for women; the "Vågö" chair by Thomas Sandell for IKEA.

companies worked with various forms of processing of Swedish raw materials. A striking number of them originated from ingenious inventions or refinements of inventions, for which Sweden has become famous. By the mid-20th century, this type of manufacturing industry had become a more important element of Sweden's export mix than raw material exports.

Even today, the traditionally Norrland-based steel and pulp/paper sectors remain highly important to the Swedish economy, accounting for around one sixth of the country's export revenues, while pure raw material exports amount to less than one tenth. What is loosely called the engineering industry accounts for an overwhelming proportion of Swedish exports, more than 50 percent. This category includes the automotive industry, telecom and electrical goods.

Global brands:
Absolut IKEA & Volvo

With only nine million inhabitants, Sweden is an insignificant market in macroeconomic terms. This is the principal reason why Swedish companies have always been extremely dependent on exports. Due to an insufficient domestic customer base, companies have simply had no choice but to look for business outside their country's borders. Early experience of international competition strengthened these companies and, in many cases, gave them a leg up on competitors from other, larger markets.

Theoretically, this is the reason why Sweden has more multinational corporations per capita than almost any other country. Volvo, Saab, Ericsson, Electrolux, ABB, Astra Zeneca, Pharmacia, Atlas Copco and SKF are only a few of these companies, all working in the manufacturing sector.

A more recent phenomenon is Swedish service and consumer goods companies that have built up strong global brands in the last few decades. The most conspicuous examples are IKEA and Hennes & Mauritz (H&M), both founded in 1947 by classic Swedish entrepreneurs and both based on the concept of making modern design available to broad segments of the population.

An exceptional case is the global marketing success of Absolut Vodka, a brand belonging to the government-owned (!) Vin & Sprit AB. By means of a brilliant design and advertising concept, Absolut managed to establish one of the world's strongest international brands in the space of only 20 years.

Future markets:
Drugs, thrills & telecom

It is often said that the future of the Swedish business sector lies in "knowledge-based industry" – high-tech, research-intensive sectors where Sweden can benefit from the high educational level of our population, our tradition of inventiveness and entrepreneurship and the general modernity of our society.

The most important of Sweden's "industries of the future" is undoubtedly the IT sector, especially telecommunications. As recently as the beginning of the 21st century, the Swedish IT miracle attracted great attention worldwide. Since then, Sweden has been especially hard-hit by "dot-com death." Meanwhile Sweden's leading export enterprise, Ericsson, underwent major difficulties due to its structural problems and a global downturn in the telecom market. Nevertheless, Sweden is well positioned in the development of cutting-edge communications technology.

Aside from IT and telecom, biomedicine is often mentioned as one of Sweden's most important industries of the future. Medical research is highly advanced in the development of new medicines and methods of treatment. In the same way as in the IT sec-

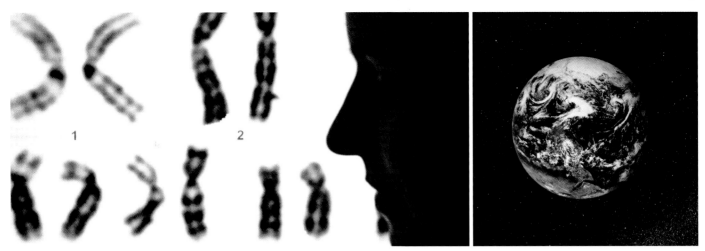

Information technology (IT) and biomedicine are considered two of the most important industries of the future in the Swedish economy.

tor, a large proportion of this development occurs in "clusters" or IT industrial parks, where private companies collaborate with leading universities, aided by central and local government investments.

In the past few years, people have spoken increasingly often of an entirely new "industry" which, together with IT and biomedicine, is counted among Sweden's economic sectors of the future. It is referred to internationally as commercial culture and includes such creative expressions as design, fashion, music, architecture and gastronomy. So successful have Swedish exports been in these fields that our political leaders have given the phenomenon its own collective label: the "experience industry." The tourist sector is also usually included in this "industry," which is expected to grow even further in importance.

Nobel:
The noblest prize

Alfred Nobel (1833–96) is internationally one of the best-known Swedes, not for his own career but for the eponymous prize created in his will.

Nobel was one of Sweden's many ingenious inventors and entrepreneurs of the late 19th century. By the time of his death in 1896, Nobel held no fewer than 355 patents, around which he had built companies in 20 countries.

Nobel was one of the wealthiest people in Sweden. He was childless and chose to give most of his assets to what came to be known as the Nobel Foundation. Nobel wanted the return on these assets to be distributed in the form of annual prizes to the individuals who had made the greatest contributions to mankind in five different fields. The fields that Nobel chose reflected

Alfred Nobel is remembered mainly for the prize that bears his name, but he was also one of Sweden's greatest-ever inventors and industrialists.

Ingenious inventions from different eras: the Celsius thermometer, color screen graphics and the adjustable wrench.

his own interests and knowledge: physics, chemistry, medicine, literature and peace, of which the first four would be awarded in Stockholm, while the Peace Prize would be awarded in the Norwegian capital of Oslo (Norway was part of a union with Sweden during Nobel's lifetime). In 1968 the Riksbank, Sweden's central bank, established a prize in economic sciences in honor of Alfred Nobel.

The Nobel Prizes, awarded for the first time in 1901, soon became the most prestigious prizes of any kind in the world. Since then, the prizes awarded in Stockholm have been presented by the King of Sweden at a ceremony every December 10 (the anniversary of Alfred Nobel's death) – held since the 1920s at the Stockholm Concert Hall, with the subsequent banquet taking place since the 1930s at the Stockholm City Hall.

Great inventions:
In ingenuity we trust

Sweden is widely known as a nation of inventors. When the names of all Swedish innovators and their inventions, improvements and discoveries are listed, it often sounds like nationalistic boasting. Nonetheless, it is remarkable how many ingenious, life-improving machines, gadgets,

appliances, systems, medicines, explanations and methods originated in our little Nordic country. The success of the Swedish business sector has largely depended – and will continue to depend – on our ability to find new methods and new solutions for a new era.

So remarkable is this phenomenon that there are numerous theories about how it came about. One of the most plausible is that Sweden is a remote, far-flung, thinly populated country with a severe climate, where in the old days it required both inventiveness and very hard work just to survive.

The history of Swedish inventions begins as far back as the 17th century with medical doctor and Renaissance man Olof Rudbeck the Elder (1630–1702), who among other things discovered the human lymphatic system. Since those days, inventions have followed more or less continuously. Below is a small selection of Swedish inventors and their most important inventions and discoveries through the centuries: Anders Celsius (1701–44), the Celsius (or Centigrade) thermometer; Carl von Linné (1707–78), *Systema naturae*, a systematic classification of plants, animals and minerals; Carl Wilhelm Scheele (1742–86), chlorine and other chemical elements; John Ericsson (1803–89), the maritime screw propeller; Alfred Nobel (1833–96), dynamite; Gustaf de Laval (1845–1913),

the cream separator; Lars Magnus Ericsson (1846–1926), development of telephone instruments and switchboards; Johan Petter Johansson (1853–1943), the adjustable wrench; Nils Gustav Dalén (1869–1937), gas-powered maritime beacons; Fredrik Ljungström (1875–1964), the steam turbine; Sven Wingquist (1876–1953), the roller bearing; Baltzar von Platen (1898–1984), the refrigerator without moving parts; Victor Hasselblad (1906–78), the single-lens reflex camera; Erik Wallenberg (1915–99) and Ruben Rausing (1895–1983), the Tetra Pak beverage packaging systems; Rune Elmquist (1906–96), the pacemaker.

Among recent Swedish inventors and their inventions are Nils Bohlin's three-point safety belt, Ericsson's digital AXE telephone switchboard stations, Håkan Lans' computer mouse, color screen graphics and GP&C system for satellite navigation, Lars Leksell's surgical Gamma Knife and Astra Zeneca's ulcer medicine Losec. In recent decades, Swedish medical researchers have also been instrumental in developing local anesthetics, intravenous nutrient delivery systems, ultrasound imaging and beta blockers for cardiovascular diseases.

The tax on private income is high in Sweden, but corporate taxes are comparatively low.

Cost of living:
Who said Sweden is expensive?

It used to be often said – and is still sometimes said – that we Swedes live under the world's heaviest tax burden. Although such comparisons are becoming more and more difficult to make, international statistics do show that Sweden is in the top ranks when it comes to the level of taxes as a percentage of overall gross domestic product. The Swedish social model is based on a general, tax-financed system of social benefits for the whole population. One consequence of this is that the Swedes pay a higher percentage of their personal income in taxes than in other comparable countries.

Less well known is that Sweden's corporate taxes, on the contrary, are low in an international comparison. Swedish companies pay a lower percentage of their income in taxes than companies in such competing industrialized countries as Germany, the United States or Japan.

Another well-established perception is that Sweden is generally an expensive country to live in. Granted, this was once true and it remains so in certain respects today. However, low inflation combined with the global currency exchange situation has changed this situation to Sweden's "advantage." International statistics comparing total living costs place Sweden today in the lower rungs among European countries. The Swedish capital, Stockholm, is less expensive to live in and visit than cities like Helsinki, Copenhagen, Oslo, London, New York, Moscow, Tokyo or Beijing. In fact, many first-time international visitors to Sweden nowadays are favorably surprised at the price picture.

The past decade has been a successful period of strong growth and good productivity gains in Sweden. The overall purchasing power of the Swedes has risen significantly, with a steadily growing, increasingly well-to-do middle class. Studies by international bodies such as the UN, the OECD and the World Economic Forum consistently show that both economically and socially, the Swedes are better off than almost any other people in the world.

Personal income tax scales (2006)

MONTHLY INCOME (SEK)	TAX (SEK)	TAX (%)
12,000	3,100	26
14,000	3,800	27
17,000	4,800	28
20,000	5,900	30
25,000	7,700	31
35,000	12,600	36
40,000	15,200	38
45,000	18,100	40

Budget for a family (2006)
Two children, aged 4 and 10. Both parents work, one of them part-time.

INCOME	SEK PER MONTH
Salary 1+2 (24,700+14,000)	38,700
Taxes/contributions 1+2	– 11,420
Child allowance	2,200
DISPOSABLE INCOME	29,480

EXPENSES	
House, 3 bedrooms	11,180
Household expenses	10,930
Child care	1,160
Car	2,900
Other	3,310
TOTAL EXPENSES	29,480

SEK 1 (Swedish krona) = approx. USD 0.14, GBP 0.07 or EUR 0.11 (September 2006)

Swedes:
Just give us a cottage
deep in the woods

In many respects, Sweden is generally considered one of the world's most modern and sophisticated civilizations. And this is true. Yet there is crucial difference between Sweden and the older cultures on the European continent. As recently as a century ago, Sweden was little more than a backward agrarian country, where a majority of the population lived under very poor conditions.

The simple rural heritage is clearly apparent in the Swedish mentality, in our sentimental relationship to nature and simplicity. It is as if we are not yet really at home in our roles as modern cosmopolitans, and as if we are constantly longing to be back in that little red cottage in the midst of a deep spruce forest. This longing is noticeable in our lifestyle, traditions and customs.

A rare combination of pronounced and sometimes extreme modernity on the one hand, and on the other hand what many foreigners regard as a surprising and exotic love relationship with our natural scenery and simple cultural heritage – this contradictory mixture embodies something that could be called typically Swedish.

National festivities:
We celebrate the change of seasons

The rural origins of the Swedes are clearly noticeable in our close, loving relationship with our Nordic natural scenery. Sometimes it seems as if the temperament of the entire Swedish national soul is determined by the dramatic changes of the seasons. The solemn, silent, dutiful winter Swede may seem an entirely different person from the jolly, outspoken bon vivant of summer. During the short and intensive Nordic summer season, it is as if for a few months, the Swedes reject modern civilization to enjoy in full measure the wonderful but ever fleeting fruits of nature. In our secularized Swedish society, this love of nature is the closest we come to a national religion.

Our national holidays and festivals all have strong elements and invocations of this nature, and of the changing seasons: Lucia in December, when processions of white-clad children holding lighted candles in their hands glide through the winter night; Christmas, when we gorge on old-fashioned agrarian winter-preserved delicacies such as pickled herring, lye-cured fish and salted ham; Walpurgis night, when bonfires are lit to symbolize driving out

Lucia, Walpurgis night and Midsummer: three national festivities that celebrate nature and the change of seasons.

winter and making way for summer; Midsummer Eve, where the peak of nature's fertility is celebrated with orgiastic intensity; the crayfish party, where the approaching autumn is defied with bright lanterns and songs under a deep golden moon in the velvety black August evening. A love of nature's wonderful treasures and a melancholy sadness over their fleetingness – these are key elements in our Swedish national soul.

Myths:
Blondes, polar bears & suicide...

When we Swedes travel elsewhere in the world, we often meet people who at first seem to have no concept of our country at all. After a while, however, it usually emerges that they actually have a few, but very firm convictions. Generally speaking, they are the same old mythical images of Sweden: a crypto-communist country populated by polar bears, dumb but willing blondes and melancholy, hard-drinking suicides. It seems as if these clichés have a life of their own. So it is just as well to "face them down," one by one:

SWEDISH SIN. This myth originates mainly in Swedish films from the 1950s, 60s and 70s with nude scenes. They have little to do with reality. It is true that the Swedes have a more relaxed attitude toward nakedness and sex than many other peoples.

However, in hard statistics about such matters as teenage pregnancies and sexually transmitted diseases, Sweden is often at the bottom in international comparisons.

Polar bears, blondes, suicide and crypto-communism are among the stubborn international myths about Sweden.

Reindeer breeding and art handicrafts are two of the three pillars on which traditional Sami culture rests. The third is the Sami language.

SOCIALISM. No, Sweden is a thoroughly democratized market economy, albeit with stronger elements of income redistribution than in many other countries.

SUICIDE. A stubborn myth, without any background in reality, which was launched in the 1950s by American right-wing propaganda as a weapon against the American liberal left, for which Sweden's "third way" policy served as a model. The truth is simply that Sweden was the first country that began to keep honest statistics about suicides (still taboo in the Catholic world and elsewhere). In fact, we are low in the international comparisons here too.

POLAR BEARS. No.

BEAUTIFUL BLONDES. Yes.

COLD CLIMATE. Yes and no. Swedish winters can be severe, but considering its northerly geographic location, Sweden has a comparatively mild climate, with a pleasantly warm summer season.

Native Scandinavians:
Sami – people of the sun and the wind

There has been a variety of opinions among historians over the years, but nowadays most of them agree that the Sami (known earlier as Lapps) are entitled to call themselves the original Scandinavians. The Sami are one of the world's smallest "indigenous" peoples. Other such groups are the Native Americans (Indians), Australia's aborigines, New Zealand's Maori and the Inuit (Eskimos) of Alaska, Canada and Greenland. The total number of Sami is estimated at 50–60,000, of whom some 15,000 live in Sweden. The Sami call their homeland Sápmi – it is a vast area covering all land north of the Arctic Circle in Norway, Sweden, Finland and the Kola Peninsula of Russia.

The main traditional livelihood of the Sami is reindeer breeding. No less than 35 percent of Sweden's total area consists of reindeer grazing land. In the old days, the Sami drove their reindeer on foot or wearing skis, with dogs as their only "employees." Today such modern equipment as snow scooters, motorcycles and helicopters is indispensable. Reindeer breeding is also counted as one of the three pillars on which Sami culture rests. The other two are the Sami language and Sami art handicrafts, using traditional materials like birch wood, reindeer hides and reindeer horns.

A group of national parks and nature reserves in Swedish Lapland are protected as unique natural and cultural treasures and included on the UNESCO World Heritage list under the collective name of Laponia (Sápmi). In the Sami language, Sami means human being. Sápmi refers both to the land of the Sami and the people who live in it. The Sami also call themselves "the people of the sun and the wind."

Royalty:
The first family

For many years, the Swedish monarchy and royal family have had only official and ceremonial functions. This does not mean that the royal family is without importance in our society. So strong is the popular support for the royal family that its position cannot really be questioned politically.

Sweden's current king, Carl XVI Gustaf, is a member of the Bernadotte family. This dynasty has occupied the Swedish throne since 1818, when Napoleon's marshal Jean Baptiste Bernadotte, "imported" to Sweden in 1810, became king under the name Karl XIV Johan. Sweden's Queen Silvia was born Sommerlath, the daughter of a German business man and a Brazilian mother. The royal couple have three children: Crown Princess Victoria, Prince Carl Philip and Princess Madeleine.

Sweden previously had male succession to the throne. This legislation was modern-

Crown Princess Victoria and Princess Madeleine; the royal couple.

Began her Hollywood career as a silent film actress in 1926. Made her sound film debut in 1930 with *Anna Christie*. Retired in 1942 and never returned to movies, despite many attempts to persuade her. Lived the rest of her life as a recluse in New York, which contributed to the proliferation of the myth.

DAG HAMMARSKJÖLD (1905–61). United Nations Secretary-General in 1953–61. Considered the most active and innovative UN Secretary-General ever. Gave the international organization a new authority. Creator of the UN's peacekeeping forces. Died in an airplane crash in what is now Zambia in 1961. Awarded the Nobel Peace Prize posthumously in 1961.

ized in 1980 to make room for Crown Princess Victoria as heiress to the throne. The crown princess, born in 1977, is currently undergoing a training program to eventually become queen.

Great Swedes

ABBA (1972–83). Its name is an abbreviation of the group members' names: Anni-Frid Lyngstad, Björn Ulvaeus, Benny Andersson and Agnetha Fältskog, four performers who comprised two couples at the beginning.

According to some sources, it is the world's most commercially successful pop group of all time, with a long succession of world-wide hits during an outstanding but short career. ABBA ended suddenly while the group was at its peak and has never reunited. Like the Beatles, ABBA then became a global brand and an industry.

GUNNAR ASPLUND (1885–1940). The biggest name among Sweden's many important modernist/functionalist architects and a leading trend-setter in Nordic modernism.

INGRID BERGMAN (1915–82). Sweden's biggest international movie star aside from Greta Garbo. Winner of three

Oscars. Caused a scandal when she left her husband and child for Italian film director Roberto Rossellini. Also a successful stage actress.

INGMAR BERGMAN (born 1918). One of the world's most influential movie and theater directors of all time. Bergman is internationally famous mainly for his psychologizing style of directing and his visual collaboration with Sven Nykvist, but he is also a great director of comedies. In recent decades, Bergman has focused mainly on his work as a stage director at the Royal Dramatic Theater in Stockholm.

BJÖRN BORG (born 1956). Sweden's greatest sportsman of all time. Revolutionized tennis with his innovative playing technique, his style on and off the court and his cool "Nordic" temperament, which gave him the nickname "Ice Borg." This clay court specialist turned in one of the most outstanding performances in sports history by winning five consecutive men's singles titles on the grass at Wimbledon in 1976–80. He won a total of eleven Grand Slam titles and then retired unexpectedly from the circuit in 1982.

GRETA GARBO, née Gustafsson (1905–90). Called "the Divine." One of the greatest movie stars and female icons of all time.

SELMA LAGERLÖF (1858–1940). Broke away from her inherited role as the genteel daughter from a manor house in Värmland province and made her debut with the major novel *The Story of Gösta Berling* (1891), based – like many of Lagerlöf's literary works – on a folk legend from her home district. Nobel laureate, 1909. First woman member of the Swedish Academy, 1914.

ASTRID LINDGREN (1907–2002). See page 3.

CARL VON LINNÉ (1707–78). See page 13.

BRUNO MATHSSON (1907–88). A prominent architect who nevertheless became famous primarily as Sweden's most outstanding furniture designer of all time.

ALFRED NOBEL (1833–96). See page 23.

OLOF PALME (1927–86). Swedish prime minister in 1969–76 and 1982–86. A radical Social Democrat who came from a wealthy bourgeois background, he was the most controversial figure in Swedish 20th century politics, both inside and outside the country's borders. Remembered mainly for his foreign policy achievements, he became one of the most prominent international advocates of Third World and small country rights and, not least, opponent of the U.S. war in Vietnam. Assassinated on an open street in Stockholm in February 1986 while walk-

Great Swedes: Greta Garbo, ABBA (Benny Andersson, Anni-Frid "Frida" Lyngstad, Agnetha Fältskog and Björn Ulvaeus) and Björn Borg.

ing home with his wife from a movie without bodyguards. No one has been convicted for the murder.

AUGUST STRINDBERG (1849–1912). Sweden's greatest-ever, most controversial writer. Even today, a dominant figure in the country's literature and cultural heritage. Was also an important painter and photographer. Throughout his career,

Strindberg was a subject of impassioned debate in Sweden. Due to constant controversies, he was never awarded a Nobel prize or elected to the Swedish Academy. Strindberg is unique in his psychological depth, power and intensity, linguistic richness and artistic versatility.

RAOUL WALLENBERG (1912–?). Swedish diplomat and a member of the country's leading

financier family. Late in World War II, with the aid of forged diplomatic passports, he saved tens of thousands of Jews in Budapest from deportation to Nazi concentration camps. Imprisoned by Soviet forces in 1945 and accused of espionage, he then disappeared. The last confirmed sighting of Wallenberg was in 1947. Today he enjoys almost saintly status, honored by monuments all over the world.

Icon Swedes

As a small nation, Sweden has not contributed many icons to our global culture. A few "Swedes" nevertheless have a tendency to pop up again and again, especially in Hollywood's image of the world...

THE VIKING. No other Nordic figure will ever come close to achieving the international fame of the Viking. More than a thousand years later, civilized Europe has yet to recover from the shock of seeing wild and woolly Northmen from a more barren clime suddenly land on the coasts of the Continent and British Isles to spread death and devastation.

THE VOLVO MAN. Have you ever wondered why those responsible and slightly boring family-supporting academics wearing tweed jackets in American films always drive Volvos? Isn't this as good a symbolic picture as any of the international image of solid Swedish reliability?

THE SWEDISH CHEF. In recent years, Sweden has distinguished itself as one of the world's most progressive gastronomic nations. But the world's most famous Swedish chef is still a muppet...

INGA FROM SWEDEN. Many modern Swedish women are frustrated that blonde, light-footed and slow-witted blondes in the world of films are so often Swedes. Amazingly often, for some reason these "Swedish" women are clad in lederhosen or other garments more reminiscent of the Alps. But then again, Hollywood has always had a hard time telling the difference between Sweden and Switzerland...

Si.
Swedish Institute

The Swedish Institute (SI) is a public agency established to disseminate knowledge abroad about
Sweden's social and cultural life, to promote cultural and informational exchange with other countries
and to contribute to increased international cooperation in the fields of education and research.
The Swedish Institute produces a wide range of publications on many aspects of Swedish society.
These can be obtained directly from the Swedish Institute or from Swedish diplomatic missions abroad,
and many are available on Sweden.se.

Sweden.se is Sweden's official Internet portal on www.sweden.se. It includes almost everything you
need to know about Sweden, ranging from basic facts about Swedish society to business issues,
politics, news, cultural life and current affairs.

In the **Sweden Bookshop** on Slottsbacken 10 in Stockholm's Old Town, as well as on
www.swedenbookshop.se, you can buy nonfiction books, brochures and richly illustrated gift
books on Sweden as well as a broad selection of Swedish fiction and children's books – in
English and many other languages – and Swedish language courses.

The Swedish Institute
Box 7434
SE-103 91 Stockholm
Sweden

Phone: +46-8-453 78 00
Fax: +46-8-20 72 48
E-mail: si@si.se
Internet: www.si.se

© 2003, 2004, 2006 Claes Britton and the Swedish Institute
The author alone is responsible for the opinions expressed in this publication.

Translation by Victor J. Kayfetz
Graphic design by Britton & Britton
Printed in Sweden by Danagårds Grafiska, Ödeshög, 2007
ISBN: 978-91-520-0751-8